Teacher's Manu

UNLOCKING
SOCIAL STUDIES SKILLS

John R. O'Connor • Robert M. Goldberg

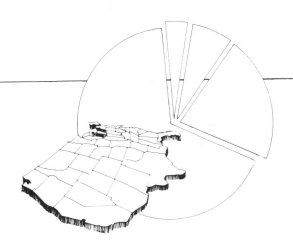

ISBN: 1-55675-687-9

Printed in the United States of America   8   7   6   5   4   3   2   1

Table of Contents

IV Research and Thinking Skills 11

Introduction

Text Organization

1. *Unlocking Social Studies Skills* is divided into four units. These units contain lessons on the following social studies skills:
    (1)   Map Skills—18 lessons
    (2)   Graph Skills—6 lessons
    (3)   Research Skills—6 lessons
    (4)   Thinking Skills—2 lessons
2. Skills are taught developmentally, from simple to the more complex. Teachers will find that the introductory exercises in some lessons will be appropriate for the ability level of some students, and beneath the ability level of others. Practices presented are those found to be most effective with students of intermediate grades who have not mastered specific skills in earlier schooling.

    Examples: students will practice with a scale of miles of "one inch to one mile" before proceeding to scales involving higher numbers or fractions; students will practice with graphs of one line before attacking the interpretation of graphs with several lines; students will practice the use of an index with few page references before they use indices with several references and cross references.

3. Each skill is introduced with an explanation of its purpose and meaning, with examples to improve understanding.
4. Students can practice each skill in the text itself. There is no need to transfer work material outside the text.
5. Practice in each skill is afforded through real and meaningful exercise material: special maps contain accurate and current data; graphs represent information on North American and world affairs; research skills deal with specific sources of information; thinking skills present actual situations.
6. The "simple to complex" gradation of exercises affords teachers the opportunity to provide for individual differences within the class.
7. In many instances, one skill is related to another, and builds upon skills previously learned. Examples: latitude and longitude are based upon practice in determining directions on a street map; an introductory circle graph uses the same information as previously shown on a bar graph; selecting proof for generalizations follows practice in supporting main ideas in research.

Text Objectives

Specific expected behavioral outcomes for each of the 32 lessons in the text are listed before the answer key to questions.

About Skills Teaching

Much of today's world is based on the principle of government by consent. We cannot predict what issues we will face or future generations will face. *Citizens must have the skills* to enable them to deal with whatever complex issues lie ahead. People must know how to *find information, interpret* it, *draw reasonable conclusions* from that information, *recognize false or emotional* information, and *reason* logically.

   In the social studies, we attempt to teach understandings, attitudes, and skills. They are related to one another. But, they cannot be taught in the same fashion. *The skills are the tools of learning.* Landmark studies in skills have concluded that it is impossible for a student to be deficient in skills and excel in the social studies.

1. **Social studies skills do not develop spontaneously.** They are not learned as a result of one's presence in the classroom each day. They are more complex than typical motor skills with which we are familiar. Social studies skills involve cognitive processes. They are more than a total of habitual responses. They are not mastered at once, and they are not learned for all time. The student is always progressing toward more mature variations of basic skills previously learned.

2. **Skills are developed through systematic instruction.** The opportunity to teach skills in their functional setting is constantly present. But skills proficiency does not result from the opportunity alone. The learner must have direct and purposeful instruction in the skills to be mastered.

3. **Practice is an essential of skills development.** Frequent practice should follow the initial presentation. Exercises in this text can form the basis for continued and motivated practice. Once the learner has achieved a functional level in the skill, practices may be less frequent. But they are necessary in order to maintain and improve the skill.

4. **Students must know when they are making progress** in acquiring a skill. Students must know what they are doing right as well as what they are doing wrong. Feedback should emphasize the positive.

5. **Skills are learned by individuals.** The exercises in this text provide for individual development and progress in each skill. Although the presentation of a skill and initial practice may be group-oriented, proficiency in the skill will vary according to the individual. Continued practice, opportunities for practice, and the nature of the practice must be provided according to individual needs.

6. **Some skills-teaching should be deferred** until students are ready to learn the skills involved. The teacher may find that some skills in the text are not yet appropriate for a particular group. Readiness to learn plays an important role in the learning process. But, one should be warned against delays in teaching a skill, lest the skill never be taught. Deferrment should result in preparation of students for instruction in the deferred skill.

7. **The teacher promotes growth in skills.** It is basic to skills instruction that the teacher know where the students are and plan instruction from that point. Too often, it is assumed that students will learn skills simply by using certain materials or taking part in class activities. Because students see maps in a text does not mean that they are using those maps correctly. Studying history does not mean that students are developing a sense of time and chronology. It is necessary to know the skill to be taught, to prepare the class for instruction, and to teach it directly.

Lesson Preparation and Answer Key

I Map Skills

1. Telling Directions

This is a basic lesson in learning directions. Students are provided with a *compass rose* for the four basic directions. They advance to one that includes the directions that lie between the four basic directions.

An exercise follows using names of "towns." Make sure that students know that the towns are make-believe. Students may proceed with the exercise at their own pace.

The next practice is an introduction to the determination of directions on a simulated *road* map. Finally, students practice finding directions on a larger map, one that is familiar to them, a map of *North America*.

If individuals have difficulty with some of the exercises, the lesson can be divided into appropriate sections for them.

Key to Lesson 1
Follow the Lines
A. 1. south 2. northeast 3. east 4. southeast
5. north 6. west 7. southwest 8. northwest
B. 1. north 2. east 3. northeast 4. east 5. south
6. southeast 7. northeast 8. west 9. northeast
10. northwest
Which Direction Is It?
1. Houston 2. Great Falls 3. east 4.a. northeast
b. east c. north d. northwest e. west f. northeast
g. northwest h. northwest

2. Directions and Places

There are two basic purposes in this lesson: (1) the introduction of a simple street map uncluttered with any other information, and (2) the introduction of the concept to be used by students in the determination of latitude and longitude.

Since streets and avenues are numbered north-south and east-west, the students will be practicing the same skill used in measuring degrees north and south, and east and west.

It ought to be made clear to students that this is not necessarily the manner in which streets are numbered in every town, although it is true in some cities.

Students are led to name avenues and streets in the first exercise. The second exercise gives further practice in naming streets through the use of *directions* and the location of specific intersections on the map.

Finally, students are asked to determine specific directions at intersections—the northeast corner, the southeast corner, etc. This may be a continuing exercise throughout the year according to individual needs. Students may be asked to label the northeast corner of their classroom, of the school, of nearby streets.

(Caution: The term *intersection* has not been used in the text. It can be used but its meaning should be explained to students beforehand.)

Key to Lesson 2
The Roads of Post
A. 1. Fourth Ave. North 2. Third Ave. North 3. Second Ave. North 4. First Ave. North 5. Central Ave. 6. First Ave. South 7. Second Ave. South 8. Third Ave. South 9. Fourth Ave. South
B. 1. Third Street West 2. Second Street West 3. First Street West 4. Main Street 5. First Street East 6. Second Street East 7. Third Street East
Finding Places in Post
A. 1. Second Ave. North 2. Third Ave. South 3. First Street East 4. Third Street West 5. Third Ave. North 6. Main Street
B.

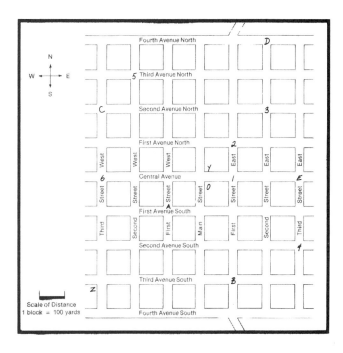

3. Using Directions to Locate Places

Knowledge of directions is reinforced with a map of the same town. However, prominent buildings and landmarks have been placed on the map. Questions posed call for:

1

1. Recognition of directions (1, 5, 7, 12, 13)
2. Interpretation of the map key (2, 4, 5, 10)
3. Giving directions through recognition of streets (2, 3, 6, 11, 13)
4. Inferring information from the map (8, 9)

Students should recognize that business areas will have the most traffic; that a street with a park, hospital, and older citizens ought to be a reasonably quiet street.

The teacher may note, for future reference, that the highway noted on the map will appear in later lessons.

Additional questions can always be posed by the teacher according to the needs of the class.

Key to Lesson 3
More About Post
1. b 2. d 3. a 4. c 5. b 6. d 7. b 8. a 9. b 10. b 11. b
12. c 13. a. bank b. gas c. police d. book store

D to F 1½ miles	D to H 1¼ miles	C to H 1¾ miles
D to E 2 miles	A to H 3¾ miles	B to J 4 miles

B.

A to B 2 miles	C to F 2 miles	D to J 8 miles
A to C 4 miles	C to G 2¼ miles	C to I 4½ miles
A to D 2½ miles	D to G 3 miles	B to F 2½ miles
A to E 4½ miles	F to G 1 mile	B to J 8 miles

C.

A to B 1½ miles	A to F 6 miles	B to J 4½ miles
A to I 3 miles	E to K 2¼ miles	C to L 5¾ miles
A to C 2¼ miles	E to M 5¼ miles	F to I 4¼ miles
A to D 3 miles	D to M 6½ miles	G to E 4¼ miles

D.

Camp to Ford: 6 miles	Camp to Lace: 10 miles
Ford to Hope: 12 miles	Clock to Sound: 6¼-7 miles
Hope to Port: 7½ miles	Lace to Sound: 13-14 miles
Hope to Save: 15 miles	Lace to Save: 22½ miles
Save to Clock: 15 miles	Hope to Lace: 15 miles
Camp to Save: 23¾ miles	

Reviewing Directions and Distance
1. northeast 2. south 3. northwest 4. 10 miles 5. 18 miles 6. 12 miles

---

4. Using the Scale of Distance

The lesson involves the simple measurement of a scale of 1 inch to 1 mile. The same skill is practiced with 1 inch equaling 2 miles, and again, 1½ miles.

The teacher may find that students can master the skill quickly. Or, it may be found that the use of a fraction in the scale presents difficulties for some students. At this point, the text may have to be set aside and instruction given in the concept of a fraction in the scale. The practice is not intended to present problems for students. However, in their future use of maps, students will encounter scales that are fractional. They should have some experience with this kind of scale. When the teacher faces the dilemma in which students may recognize the concept of the scale but have difficulty with computation, in the social studies the concept is the more important of the two.

The last practice places "towns" on a make-believe road map. This is a prelude for the lesson to follow. Approximations of distances are all that is required since "roads" are not straight lines, realistically. Students who measure distances to a fraction ought not to be penalized. The key recognizes the difficulty in accurate measurement on a road map.

Key to Lesson 4
Try It Out
A.

A to B 1 mile	F to I 2 miles	A to E 5 miles
A to C 2 miles	F to H 1½ miles	A to J 5 miles
A to D 3 miles	G to H ½ mile	C to I 2¼ miles

5. Reading a Map of More Than One Place

Many students have difficulty in recognizing that the appearance of a city, a lake, a river, will vary from map to map, according to the size of the area covered on the map. A street map of Washington, D.C., shows the city to be quite large. However, the city will occupy considerably less space on a map of Maryland and Virginia. It would be little more than a dot on a map of the United States. Students have often expressed surprise at this difference when they meet maps of different kinds.

In this lesson, students see the town of POST, which, to this point, has occupied a large amount of space on each page. Now they view POST in relation to LOCK, a larger town nearby. Questions should be posed to test students' understanding that this is the same town of POST as it appears on a map of a larger area. The teacher might show the class maps of their own town or city, a state map, a map of a province, a national map, as an aid to understanding Lesson 5.

Additional information has been added to the legend: highway numbers, water areas, main roads. The scale of miles remains at 1 inch per 1 mile. You will note that streets in LOCK are not numbered as in POST—to aid students in recognizing that there are a variety of methods used in naming streets.

Questions asked in this lesson require:

1. Recognition of relationships of smaller and larger towns (1)
2. The use of a map legend (2, 10, 13, 14, 15)
3. Ability to follow a route on a map (4, 6, 13, 14, 15)
4. Use of a scale of miles (3, 7, 8, 9)
5. Knowledge of directions (4, 5, 14, 15)
6. Ability to give directions from a map (5, 6)
7. Ability to make inferences from information on a map (11, 12)

When difficulties are located, the teacher may devise further practice through maps of his or her own design.

Key to Lesson 5
Reading a Map
1. b 2. a 3. b 4. a 5. c 6. c 7. a 8. a 9. c 10. a 11. d 12. b 13. c 14. a 15. a

---

6. Reading a Map of a State

The contents of this lesson serve as a reinforcement of concepts and skills already studied. In addition students are (1) introduced to a state map, including the towns of POST and LOCK that they have already studied, (2) given additional symbols in the map legend, and (3) asked to infer information in much the same manner as in previous lessons.

The teacher should go over the information on the map of the state of FUTURA with the class to insure that students recognize that this is a map of a larger area, a state, albeit a make-believe one. Students must understand the symbols in the legend before an attempt is made to perform the exercise.

Questions asked require:

1. Knowledge of directions (2, 7, 15)
2. Ability to use a scale of miles (1, 4, 9, 13, 14)
3. Ability to interpret a map legend (3, 4, 5, 6, 7, 8, 11, 16, 19, 20, 21)
4. Ability to draw inferences from map information (12, 13)
5. Ability to follow roads and routes on a map (10, 16, 17, 18, 19, 20)

One cannot predict how an individual class will progress through a series of developmental lessons as in Lessons 1 through 6. However, at this point, there are several skills that students have practiced. As an application of lessons learned, the class might be introduced to an actual street or road map. The same kinds of ques-

tions asked in the text can be posed for student resp .
Students should be able to tell directions, interpret ι scale reasonably, name streets and intersections, giv directions from one place to another, recognize impor· tant highways and other map symbols including buildings and water areas.

The teacher can construct test items such as are used in this text, based upon the street or road map used, to provide further practice and check the extent to which students are able to apply those skills in different situations.

Key to Lesson 6
Finding Out About Futura
1. c 2. a 3. c 4. c 5. d 6. b 7. a 8. b 9. a 10. b 11. c 12. c 13. c 14. b 15. d 16. a 17. a 18. d 19. a 20. d 21. b

---

7. Landforms

Students are provided with descriptions of some landforms both in words and on the map. The teacher should assist students in recognizing the landforms described. A verbatim definition is not a requirement. The recognition of these forms on a map is important. Many students have no conception of some landforms. To some, a mountain is the nearest piece of high ground. Filmstrips and pictures will be helpful to students in this lesson.

Practice is designed to enable students to see landforms in their own part of the world. In addition, map symbols often used to identify specific landforms are introduced. Students should be required to explain why Cuba is an island; to find peninsulas other than Florida and Alaska.

Any of the maps used in later lessons, particularly that of Europe in Lesson 15, can serve as further practice in recognition of landforms.

In Lessons 9 and 10, knowledge of land and water forms will be strongly reinforced when students are asked to make their own maps.

Key to Lesson 7
Identifying Landforms
1. see map 2. see map 3. see map 4. see map 5. western 6. ⌒ It shows the shape of mountains. 7. see map 8. see map 9. A cape is a piece of land that juts out into water; a peninsula is a larger area of land extending into water. 10. A valley is low land between mountains; plains are not surrounded by mountains.

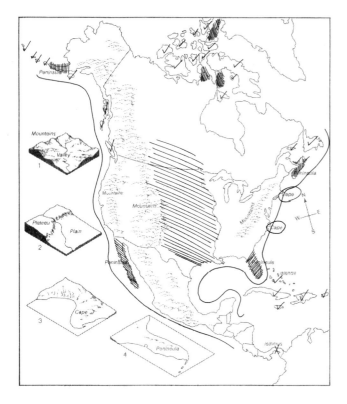

8. Water Forms

This is similar to Lesson 7. Students are given descriptions of some water forms on earth. The familiar map of Lesson 7 forms the basis for the practice. Again, filmstrips and pictures can enhance learning in this lesson.

There are some concepts regarding water forms that have proven to be difficult for students. An example is the concept of *upstream* and *downstream* on rivers. Students are accustomed to viewing maps in books, on a flat surface. Often it is not easy for such maps to give a reasonable picture of the flow of water from highland to lower land. Students can fall into the trap of believing that water flows "down" on the page. A river can flow north, and the teacher should make clear that direction does not determine the flow.

Another difficulty lies in the recognition of a *bay* and a *gulf* (sometimes a *sea*). Hudson Bay is larger in area than the Gulf of California. The Gulf of Alaska is larger than Bristol Bay. There is no clear distinction between the two terms. Students should understand that the terms have no clear cut definition that distinguishes them. Opportunities for discussion are presented in questions 6 and 10.

In both Lessons 7 and 8, the completion of the lesson by students' silent reading and answering questions may not suffice to insure learning. The teacher must lead students through a discussion of responses to exercise ques-

tions so that difficulties may be cleared before proceeding to Lesson 9.

Key to Lesson 8
Recognizing Water Forms
1. see map 2. Mississippi River 3. see map 4. 3, 2, 1, 1, 2 5. They all empty into oceans. 6. No. The Gulf of St. Lawrence is not as large as Hudson Bay. 7. see map 8. A lake is completely surrounded by land; a bay is part of an ocean. A river flows into other bodies of water; lakes are self-contained. 9. east 10. It is larger. 11. Hudson Bay and Atlantic Ocean; Gulf of Mexico and Atlantic Ocean. 12. A delta is made of tributaries that empty into a large body of water; a harbor is a small cove off a large body of water; a bay is a larger body of water usually surrounded by land on three sides. 13. Upstream means traveling against flow of the river; downstream means traveling with flow of the river.

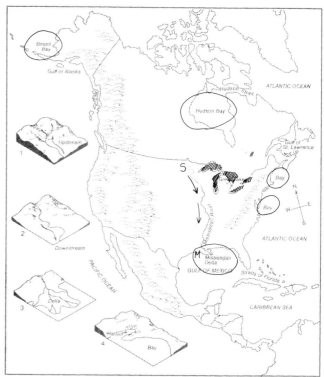

9. Land and Water Forms

This lesson is in the nature of a checkup regarding what has been studied and practiced in the two previous lessons.

A map of a mythical land is presented together with a scale of miles. The scale of 1 to 500 is used in the expectation that students will recognize the area as a continent rather than an island. Some perceptive students might suggest that it is both. The example of Australia can be used to respond to this suggestion.

Most of the land and water forms have been sufficiently isolated from one another to make recognition easier. The intent is to avoid confusion and check for identification. The forms to be identified should be recognized comfortably.

A possible difficulty—No. 13 is a cape which looks like a smaller peninsula. (Capes often do, as Cape Cod.) No. 1, however, cannot be anything else but a peninsula, so students should identify No. 13 as a cape.

Some final questions are inference questions. At this point, students should expect to "read between the lines" on a map as well as on a printed page. They have had practice in inferential questions in previous lessons. Note, too, that the river in the mythical land flows north, by intent.

Key to Lesson 9
Identifying Land and Water Forms

2 island	17 river	16 delta
12 valley	5 upstream	10 downstream
3 isthmus	6 lake	8 sea or ocean
1 peninsula	14 mountains	11 source of a river
9 harbor	15 strait	7 mouth of a river
13 cape	4 gulf or bay	18 plains

10/11. Making a Map of a Continent/ Making a Map of a State

These two lessons may be the most important of all in determining student knowledge of maps—skills, forms, and symbols.

Teachers who have used these lessons will testify to the "surprises" that may be in store when the completed projects are evaluated. However, these lessons have often been assigned to students without previous preparation. There should be fewer surprises in student responses if they have been successful in the previous nine lessons.

After students have finished Lesson 10, Making a Map of a Continent, following the recommendations in A, B, and C, they should be given an opportunity for evaluation of their own work. It is suggested that some maps—both good and poor examples—might be selected for display to the class. An opaque or overhead projector will do well for this purpose.

Ask students to compare the lake in one map with the lake in another. Are both really lakes? Where does the water come from? Compare rivers. In which direction do they flow? Do they flow from higher to lower ground? Do they empty into larger bodies of water? Examine the scale of miles. Are the scales used properly for a continent? Check the map legends. Are symbols confusing?

The same approach can be used in Lesson 11, Making a Map of a State. The scale of miles is again important if students understand the probable difference in size between a continent and a state. Section D offers reminders to students. These can be the basis for the evaluation process.

At the conclusion of Lessons 10 and 11, teachers may find it practical to repeat the assignment, or a similar assignment, focusing on errors most frequently found.

Key to Lessons 10 and 11
Answers will vary.

II More Map Skills

12. Latitude

The introduction to latitude and its meaning is almost self-explanatory in the text. Teacher assistance ought to be given, however, to insure that students again examine the method for naming avenues and streets as in the town of POST, Lesson 2. Students are given this reminder in the second paragraph. The diagram and map provide visual aids in recognizing that 90° north and south of the equator are not evident on every map. Students are called upon to identify the latitude of three places indicated in practice A.

In practice B students learn to understand the location of parallels not shown on a particular map (7° lies halfway between 6° and 8°). Inferring the direction of the equator is called for in all groups of questions.

Next, students are called upon to identify parallels that are not halfway between parallels shown on a map (11°, 18°, etc.).

The final practice of the lesson uses a combination of all steps: location of places on indicated parallels; location halfway between indicated parallels; location any distance between indicated parallels; and distance from the equator.

In marking answers in the final practice, the base should be 20 points. Direction north and south is as important as the identification of the parallels.

Key to Lesson 12
Locating Places with Latitude
A. 1. 20° N 2. 10° S 3. 30° S 4. They are both 10° north and south of the equator.
B. 1. about 7° south 2. 8° south 3. 8° south 4. 7° south 5. 7° south 6. North. Because you must go north to make the numbers decrease toward 0°.

More Practice Finding Latitude

A.

1.	A 15° South	6.	F 25° North
2.	B 10° South	7.	G 55° North
3.	C 5° South	8.	H 0° ——
4.	D 20° South	9.	O 3° North
5.	E 15° North	10.	P 11° South

---

13. Measuring Latitude

This lesson is a reinforcement of Lesson 12. Students are asked to identify the latitude of places in Latin America. This region is used because it is less familiar than North America, and it will help students in their basic knowledge of Latin America and its relationship to North America. Students should be at ease with the exercise, no matter what region is used for demonstration of that skill. As Latin America lies both north and south of the equator, 0°, it affords better evaluation of skills learned. The exercise contains a total of 30 points.

Key to Lesson 13

Practice Measuring Latitude

B.

City	Latitude	North or South
Santa Cruz	50°	South
Pôrto Alegre	30°	South
Quito	0°	——
Buenos Aires	35°	South
Mexico City	19°	North
San José	10°	North
Santiago	20°	North
Bogotá	5°	North
Cayenne	5°	North
Brasilia	15°	South
Asuncion	25°	South
La Paz	16°	South
Caracas	10°	North
Rio de Janeiro	22°	South
San Juan	19°	North

---

14. Measuring Longitude

The meaning of *longitude* can be introduced now, noting its similarities to and differences from the measurement of latitude. Latitude is cited in this lesson only as a base for understanding the measuring process in determining longitude. The lesson is concerned with longitude only.

As in Lesson 13, students are reminded of the method of naming streets in POST, Lesson 2—similar to the numbering of the meridians of the earth.

The identification of meridians (*lines of longitude* or simply *longitude* can be used with your students) is

similar to the identification of parallels. Understanding what longitude means is more important than terminology. The first exercise asks students to identify the longitude of places in the United States—a map that is familiar to them at this time. Only cities that are almost precisely on the meridians indicated, and those that lie halfway between these meridians are shown on the map. The division of degrees into minutes and minutes into seconds has not been used in this lesson. Note that in this exercise, questions are asked concerning the direction of the Prime Meridian from the United States in general, and from a specific city.

The map of the United States is followed by a map of Alaska and Northwest Canada. Determining longitudes of places in this section of North America helps students to recognize how meridians may be shown on a map of a smaller area. Students should be led to see that Alaska extends from approximately 130° West long. to 170° West long. Canada's northwestern boundary is at 142° West and extends east, beyond the scope of the map. Some of the places are not on a visible meridian, for example, Juneau, 134°; Ketchikan, 132°; and Fairbanks, 148°. Students will have to extrapolate as they have done previously in exercises on determining latitude.

Reasonable answers for the cities named above can be accepted.

Key to Lesson 14

Practice Measuring Longitude

A. 1. 100° W. long. 2. 109° W. long. 3. 91° W. long. 4. 81° W. long. 5. 80° W. long. 6. 70° W. long. 7. 80° W. long. 8. 119° W. long. 9. 90° W. long. 10. 119° W. long. 11. 76° W. long. 12. 86° W. long. 13. 96° W. long. 14. west 15. east

B. 1. 166° W. long. 2. 154° W. long. 3. 149° W. long. 4. 146° W. long. 5. 136° W. long. 6. 134° W. long. 7. 132° W. long. 8. 148° W. long.

---

15. Measuring Latitude and Longitude

Students are now ready to combine their knowledge of latitude and longitude and locate places exactly. Again, estimations are called for. These are reasonable approximations of locations and the skills demonstrated in the exercises will be all that most persons will ever need. For advanced students, teachers may wish to pursue measurements in minutes and seconds.

The practice calls for students to *name the city* at a specific latitude and longitude. Parallels and meridians are shown in units of 10°. Students will have to estimate in A only in units of 5° and 10°.

In practice B, students are required to give the *lati-*

tude and longitude of specific cities. Here, estimation will be more difficult. Example: Los Angeles at 118° W. long. and 34° N. lat. Thus, in these two exercises, students will have to read latitude and longitude to locate a city, and then identify a place through its latitude and longitude.

C, D, and E require students to know the meaning of latitude and longitude—the direction of the Prime Meridian and equator, cities east and north.

The map of Europe is used for further practice with a less familiar area of the world. The same kinds of information are called for as in A and B.

In "Comparing Information on Two Maps" the two areas are compared (the United States and Europe). Latitude and longitude are taken out of a restricted area and applied on a world basis.

Students are led to understand that:

1. Latitudinal lines have meaning in relating one part of the world with another.
2. Parts of the United States are closer to the equator than any part of Europe.
3. Some American cities are the same distance from the equator, the same latitude, as European cities.
4. Longitude helps in determining direction between continents.

Key to Lesson 15
Locating Cities in the United States and Canada
A. 1. New Orleans 2. Denver 3. Edmonton
   4. Houston 5. Chattanooga 6. Cincinnati 7. Regina
B. 1. 118° W long., 34° N lat.
   2. 88° W long., 42° N lat.
   3. 120° W long., 40° N lat.
   4. 74° W long., 46° N lat.
   5. 72° W long., 43° N lat.
   6. 93° W long., 45° N lat.
   7. 97° W long., 50° N lat.
   8. 80° W long., 33° N lat.
C. 1. east 2. south
D. 1. Chattanooga 2. Chicago 3. Cape Cod or Boston 4. Los Angeles
E. 1. Chicago 2. Montreal 3. Philadelphia
   4. Charleston
Locating Cities in Europe
A. 1. 11° E long., 60° N lat.
   2. 25° E long., 60° N lat.
   3. 14° E long., 50° N lat.
   4. 4° W long., 40° N lat.
   5. 21° E long., 45° N lat.
   6. 0° — long., 52° N lat.
   7. 30° E long., 60° N lat.

8. 10° E long., 54° N lat.
B. 1. Belfast 2. Ankara 3. Salerno 4. Reykjavik
   5. Le Mans 6. Moscow 7. Crete 8. Amsterdam
Comparing Information on Two Maps
1. F 2. T 3. F 4. T 5. T

---

16. Using a Variety of Maps

So far, the variety of maps for study has been limited. In this lesson, special kinds of maps are introduced. It is impossible in this text to give students practice with every kind of special map. In this and subsequent lessons, a few have been selected for deeper study and interpretation. The learnings acquired through practice in the next lessons can be applied to a wide variety of special maps.

Key to Lesson 16
Learning to Read Different Kinds of Maps
A. Political Maps
   1. Columbus. Map legend symbol (star in circle) for capitals 2. Springfield 3. No. The symbol of state capitals is not on Pittsburgh 4. no 5. seven 6. four 7. boundary lines, cities, and capitals of states, provinces, or countries
B. Physical Maps
   1. ⌒⌒ 2. western 3. light green 4. They are mainly in the southcentral portion of Canada. 5. Two. In the Northwest and in the Southwest. 6. dark green 7. east

---

17. Comparing Information on Three Kinds of Maps

The use of special maps in the previous lesson sets the stage for further study of special maps: *population, rainfall,* and *product*. Practice in interpretation of the message of these maps is developed as follows:

1. Reading a *population map,* based on symbols in the legend.
2. Reading a *rainfall* map, the same skill, different symbols in the legend.
3. Putting information on the maps together—getting information from the message of both maps; comparing regions according to their population and rainfall.
4. Reading a *product* map.
5. Putting information on *all* maps together.

Teachers may find that students cannot complete the entire lesson in one sitting—conditioned by the abilities of the class. If so, the lesson can be divided into two parts. The most appropriate point of separation would follow the practice on "Rainfall Maps."

Key to Lesson 17

Where People Live in the United States
1. T 2. T 3. F 4. T 5. N 6. F 7. F 8. T 9. N 10. T

Rainfall Maps
A. 1. T 2. F—40-60 3. T 4. T 5. F—Southwest
   6. F—Southeast or Northwest
B. 1. T 2. F 3. T 4. T 5. F 6. T

Mapping Farm Products
1. T 2. F 3. T 4. F 5. F 6. T 7. T

Combining Information on Three Maps
1. T 2. T 3. T 4. F 5. T 6. F 7. F

---

18. More Practice with Population, Rainfall, and Product Maps

The practice of Lesson 17 is reinforced. Population, rainfall, and product maps of Africa provide the basis for the exercises that continue the skills used in Lesson 17.

1. Interpreting a population map of Africa, using the same map symbols as in Lesson 17.
2. Interpreting a rainfall map of Africa, using the same map symbols as in Lesson 17.
3. Comparing rainfall in Africa with that in the United States.
4. Combining information on two maps—seeing the relationships between rainfall and products of Africa.
5. Comparing products raised in Africa with those in the United States.

As in Lesson 17, if the lesson cannot be completed by students in one session, a division can be made, most practically before "The Farm Products of Africa."

Key to Lesson 18

Where People Live in Africa
Check: 2, 3, 5

The Average Rainfall in Africa
1. T 2. F—less than 10 3. T 4. F—under 10 inches
5. T 6. T 7. T

Comparing Information on Two Maps
Check: 1, 2, 3

The Farm Products of Africa
A. 1. T 2. T 3. F—20-40 4. T 5. F—under 10 inches
   6. F—much 7. F—under 10 8. T
B. **Check:** 2, 4

At the conclusion of Lesson 18, your students should be able to:

1. Determine correct directions on maps of large and small areas.
2. Give directions from a street map.
3. Give specific directions at intersections of streets.

4. Follow roads and highway routes.
5. Make inferences from information on a variety of maps.
6. Use a scale of miles.
7. Approximate distances on a road map from a scale of miles.
8. Interpret symbols in a map legend.
9. Read a road map of a city or state.
10. Recognize land and water forms of the earth.
11. Construct a reasonably accurate map of a town, a state, a continent.
12. Understand and use terms associated with land and water forms.
13. Tell the latitude and longitude of specific locations on the earth.
14. Estimate latitude and longitude when parallels and meridians are not specifically indicated.
15. Compare regions of the earth through the use of latitude and special maps.
16. Interpret information on a variety of special maps.
17. Make inferences and comparisons from a variety of special maps.

III Graph Skills

19. Introducing Graphs

The study of graphs begins with a *pictograph*—probably the most lively and interesting type of graph for students. Pictographs and bar graphs have similarities, so that this lesson leads into Lesson 20 on the bar graph.

The process in the study of graphs is developmental, from the most simple relationships (one to one) to the more complex. Explanations for each of the examples and exercises ought to suffice in most instances. The explanation of the first graph may require assistance from the teacher.

Key to Lesson 19

What Is a Graph?
A. 1. Wednesday—1 gallon 2. Friday, Saturday, Sunday; Friday—5 gallons; Saturday—6 gallons; Sunday—7½ gallons 3. Tuesday and Thursday. Three gallons 4. Answers will vary.
B. 1. 4 minutes, 4 minutes, 12 minutes, 9 minutes, 5 minutes, 23 minutes, 4 minutes, 22 minutes 2. a pound of meat 3. yes 4. no
C. 1. T 2. T 3. T 4. F 5. F 6. N 7. F 8. T 9. In 1988, most immigrants came from Latin America. The fewest came from Asia.

20. Working with Bar Graphs

The introduction to the bar graph presents students with almost the same information as appeared in the previous lesson. Note that students are asked to gather information as in the previous lesson and compare these answers with those from the pictograph. Thus, they learn that similar information can be presented in different kinds of graphs. Further, if they had success with the pictographs, they will begin their practice with bar graphs with success.

In the graph on page 67, students encounter larger amounts than they had met previously. The teacher should help students to understand that the numbers at the top of the graph represent millions of barrels.

Graph C is prefaced with an example of a paragraph that might appear in a textbook or a newspaper. As a reading exercise, it may be confusing to try to remember the facts in the paragraph, but the picture is clearer when the facts are presented in the form of a graph. The main idea, the generalizations to be made, are the same in both the written passage and the graph. Here, students are introduced to a graph with *2 bars*—Graph C also demonstrates how bar graphs can show parts of a whole. (Students will see the same data in a circle graph in a later lesson.)

Key to Lesson 20
A. Reading Simple Bar Graphs
   1. Melon is two minutes less on this graph.
   2. Bar graph. No addition or counting was required; numbers of minutes was obvious.
B. 1. T 2. N 3. T 4. F 5. T 6. F
C. 1. a 2. b 3. c 4. d 5. a 6. c
D. 1. Asia 2. 58% 3. South America, Australia 4. Africa 5. all 6. Australia

21. Using Line Graphs

Practice in interpreting line graphs follows the same method as in the previous lesson—from simple to complex, as follows:
1. Explanation of a simple single line graph of a student's school average.
2. Practice with a graph of one line that steadily rises.
3. Study of a single line that shows both increases and decreases.
4. Practice with a graph of two lines—comparing two pieces of information.
5. Study of a graph with four lines, showing increases and decreases.

Key to Lesson 21
Working with Line Graphs
A. 1. F 2. F 3. F 4. F 5. T 6. T
B. 1. F 2. N 3. T 4. T 5. N 6. F 7. T
C. 1. 12 2. 12 3. 12 4. 31 5. 19 6. 1
   1. T 2. F 3. T 4. T
D. 1. all 2. Los Angeles 3. 1940 4. between 1900 and 1920 5. 1930 6. Detroit, Detroit 7. 1.2 million 8. Detroit 9. Answers will vary.

22. Circle Graphs

The circle graph most often shows parts of a whole. A simple circle graph is presented after an explanation of the resemblance of the graph to a pie. The development follows:
1. A circle graph with two parts.
2. Two circle graphs, comparing the same information in two different years: both in percentage.
3. A single circle graph with three parts.
4. A single circle graph with four parts.
5. Students construct their own circle graph given the necessary information—five parts.
6. Students interpret relationships from the graphs they have constructed.

Key to Lesson 22
Practice Reading Circle Graphs
A. 1. There was a major shift in population from country to cities. 2. Answers will vary. 3. Answers will vary. 4. 5%. 73%

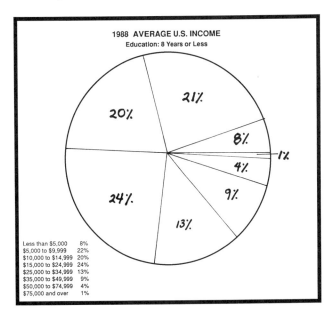

B. 1. air pollution 2. No, it is part of other, but we cannot tell what exact part. 3. 271 billion dollars 4. Yes. Water could be divided into seas, oceans, lakes, rivers, etc. Air would be divided by types of pollutants—smoke, chemicals, nuclear fallout, etc. (Other answers may vary.)

C. 1. T 2. F 3. F 4. N 5. F 6. F 7. N

Making Your Own Circle Graphs

A. 1. $15,000-$24,999 2. almost 14 3. $75,000 and over

B. 1. $35,000-49,999 2. $5,000-$9,999 3. about 42

4. More education enables a person to get higher pay.

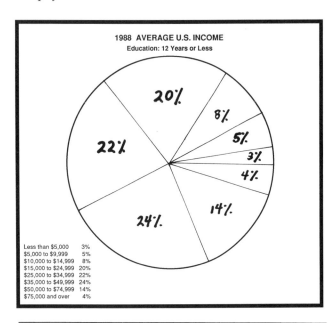

23. More Circle Graphs

This is an advanced practice with circle graphs:

1. Two circle graphs, with several parts, comparing present data and predicted data.
2. Two circle graphs of a budget comparing income and expenditures of the federal government.

The skills required are the same as learned in Lesson 22. If students are able to provide correct responses to this series of graphs, they have truly developed the skills required to handle the circle graphs they will meet in later life. More difficulty might be expected with the practice concerning the budget. Comprehension of a budget, particularly on a large scale, has proved to be difficult for some students.

Key to Lesson 23

Practice with Circle Graphs

A. 1. T 2. F 3. F 4. N 5. T 6. F 7. T 8. N 9. F

B. 1. F 2. F 3. T 4. T 5. N 6. T 7. F 8. N 9. N

At the conclusion of the lessons on graphs, your students should be able to:

1. Read and understand data presented in graph form.

2. Select important ideas and details from graphs.
3. Compare data presented on different graphs.
4. Compute information on a variety of graphs and supply missing specifics.
5. Distinguish the differences in data presented on graphs.
6. Construct a circle graph accurately.
7. Make inferences from graph information.
8. Interpret the messages presented by graphs of different kinds.
9. Generalize from information on graphs.

24. Time Lines

The purposes of a time line are explained to students in the skills text. This lesson develops the concept of a time line from a basic period of ten years through slightly longer periods, to a century, and then several centuries.

The time line is best understood through the use of boxes that represent a single year. As students progress, the boxes can be discarded, as the text does. However, the boxes ought to be retained for so long as it takes the individual student to understand the representation of a period of time.

The teacher may wish to construct time lines that provide for intermediate steps beyond those used in the text, dependent upon the progress of the class.

In the lesson, students are called upon to make judgments about specific periods of time and individual years. They not only construct time lines, they interpret them. They are asked to place information on time lines and deduce information from completed time lines. The speed with which students complete the exercises is dependent upon the successful completion of basic time line exercises at the beginning of the lesson.

Note that the final time line calls for students to understand relationships between events as well as a mere recognition of specific periods and years.

"Being Exact About Time" is intended to increase understanding of more precise language in social studies. It is also designed to develop an awareness of the indefinite and often conflicting nature of some prevalent expressions in the study of history. There are no "correct" responses in this exercise. But, students, as well as teachers, will likely be astonished at the different interpretations members of an individual class will offer for each of the expressions noted. It will also help teachers in their use of such expressions to realize that the intended meaning is not always conveyed, and most likely not to an entire class.

Teachers may prepare a chart for the summation of

student responses, and show the results to the class through the use of a transparency or overhead projector. Class responses, comments, and even suggestions should be invited.

Key to Lesson 24
What Is a Time Line?

A.

1. 1985—5 **2.** 1982—2; 1985—5; 1988

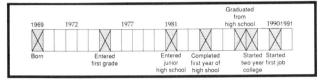

1. 1976 **2.** 1984 **3.** 1988 **4.** 1990 **5.** 4 **6.** 15
7. 1972—2; 1977—7; 1981—11; 1990—20

B. Answers will vary.
C.

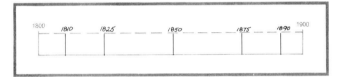

D.

E. 1. De Soto's reaching the Mississippi River
2. The founding of the Pennsylvania colony
3. Columbus reaches America. **4.a.** 1490 **b.** 1532
c. 1565 **d.** 1610

F. 1. Genghis Khan and St. Francis **2.** no **3.** about
1,000 years **4.a.** 476 **b.** 622 **c.** 800 **d.** 1095

G.

Being Exact About Time
Answers will vary.

IV Research and Thinking Skills

25. How to Use a Table of Contents and an Index

Basic to efficient and effective research is the use of a Table of Contents and Index. There will be many occasions, in and out of school, when people have to locate specific information. Knowing where to look for a possible source is but one part of the solution to the problem. Knowing which book is likely to contain the topic desired means the problem can be resolved in a minimum of time.

This lesson gives an example of how a Table of Contents can be used. Students should be able to understand the example on their own. They are given a Table of Contents containing unit and chapter titles from a mythical, but practical book. The practice calls for the selection of units and pages where specific information would most likely be located. They are asked to select the best title for a book with this Table of Contents.

In a similar fashion, the Index is explained with a sample of a partial listing. There are also samples explaining how several references for the same listing are alphabetized and the listing of cross references.

The use of the Index is developed in two stages: First, a simple Index with few additional page references and cross references, and second, an Index with a larger amount of page references and cross references. The summary exercise asks students to identify the characteristics of a Table of Contents and Index.

Key to Lesson 25
Using the Table of Contents
1. c **2.** a **3.** b **4.** b **5.** c **6.** a **7.** c **8.** a **9.** b **10.** b
Using the Index
A. 1. a **2.** a **3.** c **4.** d **5.** d **6.** b *or* d **7.** b **8.** Answers will vary: Early Cultures
B. 1. b **2.** c **3.** a **4.** c **5.** c **6.** c **7.** d **8.** a **9.** c **10.** b
C. 1. T **2.** I **3.** T **4.** I **5.** I **6.** I **7.** T **8.** T

26. Using Familiar Sources of Information

Where can a person find information about a particular topic? This lesson and those that follow will give students the opportunity to examine a variety of sources of information. This lesson is developed as follows:

1. An understanding that not all books on the same

general subject contain the same infomation, or the same amount of detail about a specific topic. There are books concerned with history that are general in scope; there are others with limited scope in terms of chronology. After a brief description of how history books, for example, may treat large or limited periods of time, students practice recognition of titles that would be most general in nature.

2. The newspaper—news articles and editorials. A news article about the financial problems of cities is followed by an editorial on the same subject. Questions ask for students to determine the main idea of each passage, to support that decision with proof, and a determination of the differences in the two, in terms of fact and opinion. (Further study of statements of fact and opinion will be a topic in the final series of lessons in this unit.)

Key to Lesson 26
How Do We Find What We Want to Know?
B. 1. *Government of the United States,* *(The Courts of Indiana)* **2.** *World Geography,* *(Geography of the United States)* **3.** *(Peanut Farming in Georgia,)* *Farm Lands of North America* **4.** *(The Colorado River, Lifeblood of the Southwest,)* *Waters of the Western Hemisphere* **5.** *(How to Give Testimony in Court,)* *The Constitution of the United States* **6.** *History of the Ancient World,* *(History of Ancient Greece)* **7.** *History of Labor Unions in the United States,* *(Women At Work in Factories)* **8.** *Water Travel in the United States in the 19th Century,* *(How the Erie Canal Changed New York State)*

A. 1. c **2.a.** Chicago stopped plans for street repairs. **b.** New York laid off 60,000 workers. **c.** Atlanta cut back on garbage collection. (Other answers are acceptable.) **3.** Answers will vary.
B. 1. b **2.** They can't afford new city halls, cars for officials, or high salaries for city workers. **3.** yes **4.** 1) City leaders haven't cared about the poor taxpayer. 2) Taxpayers cannot or will not give more. 3) City officials must give something back to their people. (Other answers acceptable.) **5.** The news article gives more facts, the editorial more opinion. **6.** news article **7.** Answers will vary.

27. Magazines and Encyclopedias

The lesson examines other sources of information met in research—the *Reader's Guide to Periodical Literature* and the encyclopedia. This lesson includes:

1. A sample listing from the *Reader's Guide* in which the code for the guide is unlocked—each item in a listing is explained.
2. Practice in locating information from a sample listing of the *Reader's Guide.*
3. A description of what encyclopedias are, and how information is organized.
4. Practice in extracting the most likely sources for specific information in the listed volume of an encyclopedia.

Most students become familiar with an encyclopedia of some kind before most other research materials. The organization of topics may be familiar to them. Some may never use the *Reader's Guide to Periodical Literature,* despite its usefulness as a research tool. Teachers should bring samples of the *Reader's Guide* to class and allow students to examine them. When classes visit the library, they should be shown the location of the *Reader's Guide* in the Reference section.

Key to Lesson 27
How to Find Magazine Articles
1. S.D. Lewis **2.** 2, several in 3, 4, 6—1st entry **3.** five **4.** Reader's Digest **5.** Feb., 1978 **6.** monthly **7.** Energy and the Dollar **8.** pages 47–49 **9.** one—page 56 **10.** Energy and the Dollar **11.** U.S. Energy Demand and Supply **12.** Energy Conservation *or* Facing Up to Reality
Using the Encyclopedia
1. c **2.** a **3.** a **4.** d **5.** b **6.** c **7.** b **8.** a **9.** c

28. How to Use an Atlas and an Almanac

It is not possible in a text of this nature to give students an accurate view of the breadth of variety of maps, diagrams, charts and facts contained in an atlas. But, it should not be overlooked as a research tool. Students should have the opportunity to examine the atlas in the classroom and library. Students should be taught the special skills in using the index of the atlas.

The almanac is a reference tool for all citizens. Students most often do not know all the interesting facts that an almanac contains. It is unsurpassed for current factual data in a wide variety of topics. Lesson 28 attempts to acquaint students with this research tool. The selected items from an almanac should provide students with a view of the variety of topics on one small part of the index.

The final set of questions in this exercise is an application of this and previous lessons. It is a check on learning—do students know the kind of information they would find in the almanac and encyclopedia? Which is probably more current? In which are there lists of facts and records? Which is more detailed in its explanations?

Key to Lesson 28

What Is an Almanac?

A. **1.a.** photography **b.** Ping-pong **c.** pole-vaulting
   2.a. Franklin Pierce **b.** Francisco Pizarro **c.** Edgar A. Poe **3.** pp. 430–432 **4.** pp. 192, 218 **5.** p. 388 **6.** p. 90 **7.** pp. 754–56

B. **1.** A **2.** E **3.** A **4.** A **5.** E **6.** A **7.** A **8.** E

---

29. Interpreting Information

"You can't believe everything you read," may be advice for Lesson 29. The lesson is based on actual examination of seven history textbooks in use in junior and senior high schools. It attempts to teach students that:

1. All the information about a topic will not be found in one source.
2. Even textbook authors have different ideas about which events or persons in history are most significant.
3. Even if writers agree on the importance of an event, they will differ on the amount of space it should be given in a textbook.
4. People are governed in reporting by their own points of view, biases perhaps.

The study is in the form of a chart revealing the amount of space each of seven texts allots to four different people and their roles in American history. The chart reveals a wide variety in coverage in the texts. The questions propose to lead students to understand that there must be reasons for the disparity in coverage of the events shown in the chart.

"Which One Would You Use?" provides a further checkup of the extent to which students understand the purpose and organization of five sources of information studied in the lessons on research skills.

Key to Lesson 29

What's Important?

1. George 2. Charlie 3. only one 4. three 5. George
6. McCarthy, Carnegie 7. Perry, Sojourner 8. Sojour-

ner 9. Carnegie 10. McCarthy 11. Answers will vary.
12. Answers will vary. 13. Answers will vary.
Which One Would You Use?
1. D 2. B 3. E 4. A 5. B 6. C 7. D 8. C *or* A 9. C
10. A 11. A 12. E 13. B 14. D 15. C

---

30. Making a Summary of Your Research

Taking notes and writing or giving an oral report is a necessary part of research. Lesson 30 provides a formula for these skills. This lesson is only the beginning of the practice. Students should be taught to follow a procedure similar to the one described every time they research a topic for class reporting.

The method is simple: select main ideas and support these ideas. This is not the total picture of performing research. Ideas eventually have to be combined under more general headings—and in larger reports, sections and chapters have to be added. But, this lesson is a basic one. In reading, in listening, or in viewing a film, students should form the habit of determining which are the important ideas, noting several facts in support of each idea, and then forming the body of the report.

A sample magazine article and the subsequent exercise give basic practice in the procedure described.

Key to Lesson 30

Practice Summarizing Your Research

A. Main Ideas, Paragraph 1
   In the Soviet Union there are political prisoners.
   (We know little about Soviet labor camps.)
   Supporting Statements
1. The Soviet Union does not give information about prisons, the number of prisoners, or their treatment.
2. Their crimes are those of speaking or writing unfavorable things about the Soviet government.
3. Others may have spoken out about the treatment of minorities in the Soviet Union.

B. Main Idea, Paragraph 2
   Prisoners cannot speak out for their rights.
   Supporting Statements
1. If prisoners say nothing, they can live through the hardships.
2. If they speak out . . . they can receive even harsher treatment.
3. They can be placed in a dark dungeon . . . and lose mail and visiting privileges.

C. Main Ideas, Paragraph 3
   Keeping prisoners hungry seems to be part of the Soviet plan.

Supporting Statements

1. Another said that he never ate enough.
2. Experts who have studied statements of former prisoners believe that keeping people hungry is part of the punishment.
3. Former prisoners say that prison meals would have enough food for a child of nine.

D. Main Idea, Paragraph 4

Prisoners are forced to live under inhumane conditions.

Supporting Statements

1. She lived with twenty-three other women in a room ten feet by twenty feet.
2. No one had time to wash in the morning.
3. It was possible to take a bath once every ten days.
4. Relatives could visit every fourth month.

(Throughout, other answers are acceptable.)

---

31. Generalizations

Generalizations result when a set of facts is combined into a summary statement, the important idea. We often make judgments through generalizations we accept rightly or wrongly. In this lesson, students are lead through a series of examples to understand that to generalize is to summarize that which most often occurs. Rarely can we make a generalization covering every circumstance. Hopefully, students will learn that a generalization is a summary of what happens generally, most often, is likely to occur, can be predicted if the unusual does not take place.

Through the examples shown, students can be led to see that a generalization is most often the *main idea* of a set of facts (whether or not in paragraph form), the *summary* statement, the *conclusion* that can be drawn from a set of facts.

In the first practice, students are given a choice of generalizations from a set of facts and then later, are asked to supply their own generalizations from facts given.

Exercise C affords students an opportunity to avoid the sweeping generalizations, often a stereotype. It can be called an exercise in open-mindedness. Nearly all statements call for "some" or "most" as a response.

In an exercise of this type, *many* and *a few* are sometimes offered as choices. This results in some difficulty in determining the most appropriate response in many cases. Teachers should go over responses with the class, and may elect to ask whether "many" or "a few" is a better response than "some" or "most."

It is hoped that participation in this exercise will enable individuals who are prone to making sweeping generalizations avoid them thereafter.

Key to Lesson 31
What Is a Generalization?
A. 1. b 2. a 3. a 4. c 5. b
B. 1. The East has many large cities with fine harbors. 2. There are great oil-producing countries in every continent. 3. Old and modern customs are a part of North African village life. 4. All presidents have been men and most are well educated and come from states with large populations. 5. People in low income brackets are most often the victims of crimes.
C. 1. Some 2. Some 3. Most 4. Some 5. Some
6. Some 7. No 8. Some 9. Some 10. Some
11. Some *or* Most 12. Some 13. Most
14. Some 15. Some 16. All 17. Some 18. Some
19. Some 20. Some

---

32. How to Supply Proofs for Statements or Generalizations

This is a followup to the previous lesson. Students are now given generalizations and asked to select appropriate proofs or supporting statements for each. The examples provide students with practice in selecting supporting statements for generalizations that are within the scope of their experience. Explanation of the rationale for correct supporting statements is presented in the text.

There are four correct responses in the exercise. The number of blanks is a clue to the student regarding the number of correct responses for each generalization. Teachers may wish to go over responses with the class, particularly if there are a greater number of incorrect selections of proofs than anticipated.

Key to Lesson 32
Practice Finding Proofs
1. b, c 2. b, d 3. b, c 4. a, c, d 5. b, d 6. a, b, d 7. c, d
8. b, c 9. a, d 10. b, c, d 11. a, b 12. a, c
At the conclusion of Lessons 25–32, students should be able to:

1. Use a Table of Contents effectively.
2. Use an Index, including items with several references.
3. Locate information through cross-references in an Index.
4. Distinguish which, from among several books,

is the one most likely to treat the topic of interest.

5. Contrast information in an editorial and a news article.
6. Select personal opinions in written material.
7. Locate articles of interest in the *Reader's Guide to Periodical Literature.*
8. Select appropriate information in an almanac.
9. Recognize differences between a variety of sources of information.
10. Make inferences from sources of information.
11. Identify differences among experts' views of the importance of persons and events in history.
12. Use more than one source to find information about a particular reference.
13. Take notes and organize them in making a report.
14. Make summary statements from a set of facts by seeing relationships among the facts.